# The Adventures of Selena the Seashore Bench

By Nedia Lee

Hi, I am Selena the Seashore Bench.
Come join me for a beautiful day at the beach.
I wonder what we will see....
I am not sure, but I know we will be able to talk to our family and friends about our new adventure.

Let us begin our journey at the beach.

The first thing I see is the sun peeking over the horizon. This is called a sunrise. The sky has beautiful red, yellow and orange tones.

Have you seen other colors in the sky when the sun is rising?

While the sun is rising, it shines bright on the water. When the light hits the waves, the water looks like glitter.

I see many sparkles in the water. Do you see all the sparkles?

SWASH....SWASH....SWASH....

The waves hit the beach over and over. When this happens, it is called a receding wave.

The highest part of a wave is called the crest. The lowest part of a wave is called the trough.

Can you count the waves?

Sand....Sand....Sand.....Sand is everywhere!

The beach is full of sand. This sand is a pale cream color.

Did you know that sand can be different colors?

Some sand around the world can be red, brown, pink, purple, orange, green, gold and even black.

What is your favorite color of sand?

I see seashells in the sand.

Shells are hard and are usually created by animals that live in the sea. They protect the body of the sea animal. They come in different colors, shapes and sizes.

Seashells.....seashells.....and more seashells!

Shells help our ecosystem. It is better to leave seashells on the seashore.

How many different types of seashells do you see?

The first to arrive at the beach are the lifeguards. Their job is very important.

Lifeguards rescue people and animals when they are in trouble. They make sure everyone is safe and are following all the rules. They can also provide first aid.

When ever you get a chance,

you should always thank a lifeguard.

Oh my goodness! I see a dog playing with the seashells!

It's our first family of the day joining us at the beach. I think the dog is their pet. They are setting up their area for a great day at the beach. They set up their beach chairs, umbrella, towels and their cooler. They even brought some beach toys.

Let's see what fun things they have planned.

The first thing they do is put sunscreen on their face, arms and legs. This protects their skin.

After everyone has sunscreen on, they begin to walk on the beach.

Have you ever walked on a beach? How does the sand feel under your feet?

When they come back from their walk, they begin to build a sandcastle.

They are making sure they don't build it too close to the water.

Sandcastles can be many shapes and sizes. You will need tools like buckets and shovels.

The most important thing to remember when building a sandcastle is to have fun….fun…..fun….

It looks like they are ready to get in the water.

SPLASH! SPLASH! SPLASH!

They are having so much fun in the water.

Some are swimming.

Some are playing with a ball.

Some are just sitting in the water and enjoying the small waves.

Remember these tips for staying safe in the water:

Stay close to the shore and never wonder out too far.

Never be alone in the water.

Always pay attention to your surroundings.

Make sure there are no jellyfish or sharks, If you see these two things, get out of the water.....

It is getting close to lunchtime. Mom and dad begin to prepare lunch for their family.

They have sandwiches, chips, water and Kool-Aid.

The food is ready!

Come and get it!

The children come running out of the water to have lunch together with their mom and dad.

Oh no! Watch out!

Seagulls begin to fly above them. Seagulls live near the sea because their main food is fish, but they love your beach snacks.

The family begins to throw food up to the seagulls.

Be careful because seagulls like to swoop down and steal your food.

Did you know that if you stare at them, they will not swoop down?

There are other types of animals
you can see at the beach.

I see a pelican. Do you see a pelican?

I see a turtle. Do you see a turtle?

I see a sea snail. Do you see a sea snail?

What other types of animals have you seen
at a beach?

Well, the family has finished eating and begin to pick up all their trash.

It is very important to keep the beach clean. Always remember to clean up after yourself and throw the trash away where it belongs.

Everyone seems a little tired. They place their towels on the sand to sunbathe.

Some of them are sitting and some are lying down, but they are all together with their dog.

This is relaxing, but you should not do this for a very long time.

While the family is sunbathing, I notice a boat far out in the ocean. I think the people on the boat are fishing.

I hope they catch some fish! Yummy, yummy in my tummy.....

Have you eaten fish before?

It's getting late. The family has started to pack up to go home.

I hope they don't forget anything.

Hey family…..don't forget your dog!

It is time for the sun to leave us. It begins to disappear below the horizon. This is called a sunset. The sunset looks even more beautiful with the clouds all around.

WOW.....it looks magical......

Now that the sun is setting, guess what animal begins to come out? You guessed right!

Crabs....crabs....and more crabs!

There they come....scooting across the sand. They love coming out at night.

OH LOOK!

Some crabs are walking up to me. I think they want to be my friend.

Did you know that crabs can walk forwards and backwards? Some can even swim.

I'm going to ask them to stay with me all night. I love spending time with them.

I hope you enjoyed our adventure at the beach. If you are looking for another adventure, look for my friend, Freddy. He is Freddy the Farm Bench. If you like farm animals, get ready for Freddy.

Bye, bye....

www.ingramcontent.com/pod-product-compliance
Lightning Source LLC
Chambersburg PA
CBHW041709160426
43209CB00017B/1781